ISRAELI

COOKBOOK

ISRAELI COOKBOOK

65 of the Best, Beginner-Friendly, Delicious, Easy-to-Follow, and Ingredient-Accessible Recipes in Israeli Cuisine

NAOMI HOFFMAN

CONTENTS

INTRODUCTION

I want to thank you for choosing Israeli Cookbook. I hope you find the book helpful in your quest to master Israeli cooking.

People feel connected to Israel for various reasons, but its cuisine ranks high up in the likeability meter. Israel is home to some amazing dishes that embody a gastronomic and cultural flavor. Israeli cuisine has been adapted over the centuries, and some of the best dishes have traveled to numerous countries. These recipes represent some of the most inventive and delicious combinations of vegetables, cheeses, spices, fruit, meat, and other ingredients. It is for this reason that Israeli cuisine is a collection of flavors.

It was after the Second World War that the Israeli cuisine gained fame. After WWII, a lot of sympathy was generated toward the Jews. People believed that there should be a Jewish homeland to save the displaced Jews, the victims of the Holocaust who were left to die in Europe. David Ben-Gurion, the founder and first prime minister of Israel, declared Israel to be independent in 1948. Both America and Soviet Union recognized the new state.

THE EMERGENCE OF A NEW CULINARY PICTURE

The face of Israel changed, and a new culinary picture slowly began to emerge. Many enemies surrounded the infant state, which continued to absorb over 100,000 immigrants every year. The wave of immigrants was not only made up of Jewish people who were displaced due to the Holocaust, but also the Jews from Middle East. Different styles of cooking and eating emerged when Jews from different parts of the Middle East moved to Israel.

The increasing number of immigrants did cause a strain on the economy. It was between the years 1948 and 1958 that the people in Israel had to ration food. Women cooked with wild greens that they collected from the field, and new ingredients, such as couscous, were introduced into the diet. These new foods satisfied the needs of people from different cultures. Some vegetables, such as eggplant, were used as a substitute for meat. Soon, the canning industry in Israel began to supply canned tomato puree and paste, tahini, hummus, and mayonnaise in tubes.

There was, however, one issue that needed to be resolved in the new country, and this law was the position on the dietary laws. Ben-Gurion chose to continue with the status quo agreement and decided to continue with the rabbinical supervision of the dietary laws of kashrut (kosher eating laws) in all hospitals, schools, military service, and government organizations. The rabbis also had to compromise. The United States government sent millions of pounds of preserved food through the Agency for International Development. They sent dried skim milk, dried eggs, butter, cheddar cheese, and dried codfish. The rabbis in Israel had to verify if the cheese was kosher before they could consume it. It was only when Maury Atkins, who worked in the American embassy, confirmed that the cheese was the most wholesome cheese that was sold in the United States, but it could include a small percentage of non-kosher animal product. The Chief Rabbi agreed that children, until the age of 14, could eat cheddar cheese.

Meat that was kosher was also scarce. Most meat was imported from Romania and Palestine before the war. It was only after the war that the meat was supplied from Argentina, Brazil, and Uganda. The Israelis could obtain kosher beef from the male calves produced from herds that were rapidly growing because of dairy cows. It was only when the water sources improved in the late 50s that large herds of cattle (produced for beef) were introduced into the agricultural economy in Israel.

THE DIVERSITY

When the fertility of the land increased, the excitement to create new dishes and food to meet the needs and desires of the growing population also increased. The author of Fruits Grown in Israel, Shaul Homsky, stated that Israel is a unique state. The climate in a small area close to the Sea of Galilee is subtropical, and this is where kiwis, bananas, and mangoes grow. In the mountains of Golan and Galilee, the temperature was ideal for the growth of apples and cherries.

The constantly changing population has had a significant effect on Israeli agriculture. The population in Europe was accustomed to eating plums, cherries, and apples, while the population from the Middle East loved to eat dates, grapes, and olives. Since there were no agricultural traditions that were transferred from one generation to the next, farmers were always willing to learn. They were ready to experiment with new techniques and also with new vegetables and fruit. This state was unlike Greece, where generations of farmers followed the same techniques and methods.

The experiments did not always work. For example, the minister of agriculture, Moshe Dayan, introduced a cylindrical, thick-skinned, juiceless, and tasteless tomato as a substitute to the Marymont, Israel's favorite. Dayan believed that this vegetable would be cheaper to produce and would make more money. He also believed that this vegetable would appeal to different countries that imported from Israel. It was for this reason that farmers were asked to grow the new vegetable. This experiment was a failure, and most people in Israel believed that this was Dayan's way to assault the farmers in Israel.

New vegetables and fruit had a lot of presence in the market, and many chefs were excited about taking advantage of the novelty of these ingredients. Over the course of the years, different chefs experimented on different types of food, and this led to the new Israeli cuisine that people across the globe have come to know and love.

If you love food from different parts of the world, then you can bring the smells and savory tastes of Israeli cuisine into your home through these delectable recipes. This book has some of the best and authentic Israeli recipes that are easy to make. The ingredients used for these recipes can be easily sourced from your local supermarket. All ingredients are pocket-friendly, which makes cooking Israeli food affordable. These recipes are so easy that even someone who is still learning the basics of cooking can try them. I hope you and your family enjoy the delicious recipes in this book.

CHAPTER 1

ISRAELI CONDIMENT, DIP, AND SPREAD

ZA'ATAR SPICE MIX

Makes: ¼ cup

Ingredients:

- 1 tablespoon dried oregano
- 1 tablespoon sesame seeds
- ½ tablespoon dried thyme (thyme is also called as za'atar)
- 1 tablespoon sumac
- ½ tablespoon dried marjoram
- ½ teaspoon fine sea salt

Directions:

1. Gather all the ingredients and place them in a skillet. Toast lightly. Remove the skillet from heat and let it cool completely before adding it into a jar.

2. Place the jar at room temperature. It can last for 4-5 weeks.

JERUSALEM SPICE MIX

Makes: ¼ cup

Ingredients:

- ¼ teaspoon + 1/8 teaspoon ground cinnamon
- ¾ teaspoon ground cardamom
- ¾ teaspoon curry powder
- ¾ teaspoon ground coriander
- 1 ½ heaping teaspoons crushed garlic
- ½ teaspoon paprika
- ¾ teaspoon turmeric powder
- A pinch ground cloves
- ¾ teaspoon ground pepper
- 2 ¼ teaspoons sumac powder
- 1 ½ teaspoon kosher salt
- 3/8 teaspoon chili powder

Directions:

1. Add all the ingredients into a spice grinder. Blend until finely powdered.

2. Transfer into a small glass jar. Fasten the lid and store it in the refrigerator until use.

BAHARAT SPICE MIX

Makes: About 1/3 cup

Ingredients:
- 2 tablespoons black peppercorns
- 1 teaspoon ground cinnamon
- 2 teaspoon coriander seeds
- ¼ teaspoon ground nutmeg
- ½ teaspoon cardamom seeds
- 1 teaspoon whole cloves
- 1 tablespoon cumin seeds
- 1 ½ tablespoon paprika

Directions:
1. Heat a pan on medium heat. Add peppercorns, coriander, cloves, cumin, and cardamom to the pan.

2. Roast until it becomes aromatic, should be around 2-3 minutes. Turn the heat off and allow it to cool.

3. Transfer into a spice grinder. Add paprika as well and grind until smooth.

4. Store the spice mix in a small glass jar at room temperature.

HAWAIJ SPICE MIX

Makes: 1 cup

Ingredients:

- ¼ cup freshly ground black pepper
- 1 tablespoon ground coriander
- 2 tablespoons turmeric powder
- 1 tablespoon ground cardamom
- ½ cup ground cumin

Directions:

1. Add coriander, turmeric, cardamom, and cumin powder into a small pan. Place the pan over low heat.

2. Stir frequently and toast until it gets aromatic. Turn off the heat.

3. Add pepper and stir. Let it cool completely.

4. Store in a small glass jar at room temperature.

HUMMUS

Makes: About 2 cups

Ingredients:

- 1 cup dry chickpeas, rinsed, soaked in water overnight
- 4 tablespoons tahini paste
- 2 cloves garlic, peeled, chopped
- Paprika to taste
- ½ teaspoon baking soda
- Juice of a lemon
- ½ teaspoon salt or to taste
- A handful fresh parsley, finely chopped, to garnish
- Extra-virgin olive oil, to drizzle

Directions:

1. Add chickpeas into a pot or instant pot or pressure cooker after draining and rinsing.

2. Pour enough water into the pot such that the chickpeas are covered with water and about 2 inches above the level of chickpeas.

3. Place the pot over high heat. Reduce the heat when it starts boiling.

4. Discard scum if visible. Cover and cook until soft. It can take a long time, so it is preferable to cook them in a pressure cooker. Once cooked, the chickpeas should crush easily when pressed.

5. Retain about ½ cup of the cooked liquid and discard the rest.

6. Retain a handful of cooked chickpeas and add the rest of the chickpeas into the food processor bowl. Add tahini, the retained liquid, garlic, pepper, salt, paprika, and lemon juice and blend until smooth.

7. Taste and adjust the lemon juice or tahini if required.

8. Transfer into a serving dish. Drizzle olive oil on top. Garnish with parsley and retained chickpeas.

9. Sprinkle some paprika on top and serve.

10. Store leftovers in an airtight container. Refrigerate until use.

AMBA (PICKLED MANGO SAUCE)

Makes: 26-30 ounces

Ingredients:

- 1 ½ pounds large, firm, raw mangoes, peeled, cubed
- 1 ½ tablespoons oil
- 2 small Fresno chilies, deseeded, finely chopped
- 3 cloves garlic, peeled, minced
- ½ tablespoon ground turmeric
- 1 teaspoon ground coriander
- Cayenne pepper to taste
- 1 ½ tablespoons kosher salt
- 1 teaspoon mustard seeds
- 1 teaspoon ground fenugreek
- 1 teaspoon ground cumin
- 1 ½ tablespoons brown sugar or to taste
- ¼ cup white vinegar
- ½ cup water

Directions:

1. Place mango in a glass bowl. Sprinkle salt over it and mix well.

2. Cover and chill for 24 hours. Stir occasionally.

3. Place a pot over medium-low heat. Add oil. When the oil heats, add mustard seeds. When the spluttering begins, add garlic and chili and stir for 60-80 seconds until garlic is light brown and aromatic.

4. Stir in all the spices and cook for a minute stirring constantly.

5. Stir in brown sugar, mango, and water. Raise the heat to medium heat.

6. Cook until mangoes are soft, stirring frequently.

7. Taste a little of the mixture and add more of the spices, sugar, salt, or vinegar to suit your taste if desired. Turn off the heat.

8. Blend the mixture with a stick blender until most of it is smooth with a few chunks of mango.

9. Let it cool completely. Spoon into jars. Ensure that the lids of the jars are tightened and the jars are placed in the refrigerator. It can stay fresh for about 18-20 days.

TAHINI PASTE & TAHINI SAUCE

Ingredients:

For tahini paste:
- 2 cups sesame seeds, hulled
- ¼ cup olive oil or more if required
- Salt to taste (optional)

For tahini sauce:
- 1 ½ cups lukewarm water
- 2 cups tahini paste
- Salt to taste
- 6 cloves garlic, peeled, minced
- ½ cup fresh lemon juice or to taste
- 2 teaspoons minced parsley

Directions:

1. To make the paste: Heat a heavy skillet over medium heat. Add sesame seeds. Stir frequently until they start popping lightly (you can hear a slight sound if you listen carefully).

2. Stir constantly until they are light golden brown. Turn off the heat. Set aside to cool.

3. Place the sesame seeds in a food processor. Add olive oil. Blend to make a paste. Add more oil if the paste is too thick and blend again.

4. Store in an airtight jar in the refrigerator. It can be stored for many months. Use tahini sauce or tahini paste, depending on what is mentioned in the recipe.

5. To make tahini sauce: Place garlic, tahini paste, lemon juice, water, and salt in a blender and blend until smooth. If you find the sauce very thick, add some more water and blend until you get a smooth sauce. Thick sauce is used for making hummus, while thinner sauce is used for using tahini sauce as a dip.

6. Transfer into an airtight container. Add parsley.

7. Refrigerate until use. It can store for up to 5 days.

SCHUG OR ZHUG

Makes: About 1 cup

Ingredients:

- 5 whole jalapeño peppers, deseed if desired
- 1 cup chopped parsley
- 1 cup chopped cilantro
- 4 cloves garlic, peeled
- ¼ teaspoon ground cardamom
- A large pinch ground cumin
- 1 tablespoon extra-virgin olive oil or more if required
- ½ teaspoon salt or to taste
- ¼ teaspoon caraway seeds (optional)
- A bit of black pepper

Directions:

1. Place all the ingredients in the food processor bowl. Give short pulses (2-3 seconds each) until well-combined and rough in texture.

2. Add more oil if the mixture is too dry.

3. Spoon the mixture into an airtight container and place the container in the refrigerator. It can last for about 5 days.

CHOCOLATE SPREAD

Makes: 3 cups

Ingredients:

- 2 cups oil
- 2 cups sugar
- 14 egg yolks
- 5 tablespoons cocoa powder

Directions:

1. Place all the ingredients into the mixing bowl of the stand mixer. Set the mixer on medium speed and beat until incorporated and smooth.

2. Pour the mixture into a heat resistant bowl. Use the double boiler method over low heat. Cook until thick. Stir every 5-6 minutes.

3. Remove the bowl from the double boiler and cool completely.

4. Transfer into an airtight container.

BABA GHANOUSH

Makes: About 3-4 cups

Ingredients:

- 2 large eggplants
- 4 cloves garlic, minced
- 4 tablespoons lemon juice
- 4 tablespoons tahini paste
- Salt to taste
- 4 tablespoons extra-virgin olive oil
- 2 tablespoons chopped fresh parsley
- Sumac powder for garnishing (optional)

Directions:

1. Pierce eggplants all over with a fork.

2. Take a rimmed baking sheet and place the eggplants on it.

3. Preheat the oven and roast the eggplants at 400° F for 45 minutes or until tender inside. Turn the eggplants every 10-12 minutes.

4. When the eggplants are roasted well, take out of the oven and allow them to cool. Peel the charred skin and discard.

5. Place the eggplant, garlic, lemon juice, tahini, and salt in a food processor. Blend until slightly chunky or the texture you desire.

6. Transfer on to a serving bowl. Sprinkle sumac powder on top if using it.

7. This can be used as an appetizer or for filling in sandwiches or as spreads.

LABNEH (YOGURT CHEESE WITH HERBS)

Makes: About 2 cups

Ingredients:
- ½ tablespoon minced, fresh herbs (such as mint, thyme, chives, or parsley)
- 1 cup extra-virgin olive oil
- 16 ounces yogurt
- Salt to taste
- Pepper to taste (optional)

Directions:
1. Place yogurt on a large piece of cheesecloth. Bring the ends of the cloth together and tie it with a string.

2. Hang the cheesecloth at some safe place, at room temperature. Keep a bowl below the cheesecloth to collect the drippings. This is for sour cheese. Let it remain this way for 24 hours.

3. For plain cheese (not sour), place the cheesecloth in a colander placed over a bowl. Place the entire thing in the refrigerator for 24 hours.

4. Remove the cheesecloth and transfer the cheese into a jar. Add seasonings and herbs and stir well. Drizzle oil over it. Close the lid of the jar. Place the jar in the refrigerator and use it within a week.

5. The collected liquid is called whey and can be used in some other recipe, such as a smoothie or pickles.

TZATZIKI SAUCE

Makes: About 1 ¼ cups

Ingredients:

- 9 ounces full-fat Greek yogurt
- 2 small cloves garlic, peeled, minced
- ½ tablespoon chopped fresh mint leaves
- 1 tablespoon olive oil
- 5 ounces cucumber, finely minced
- Salt to taste
- 2 teaspoons white wine vinegar

Directions:

1. Line a strainer with cheesecloth. Add yogurt into the strainer placed over a bowl. Place this entire thing in the refrigerator. Let it drain for 2 hours. The collected liquid is called whey and can be used in some other recipe, such as in a smoothie or pickles.

2. Meanwhile, place cucumber in another fine wire mesh strainer. Add about ½ teaspoon salt and toss well. Place the strainer over a bowl to collect the drippings. Let it sit for 10 minutes.

3. After 10 minutes, squeeze the cucumber of excess moisture. Transfer the cucumber into a bowl.

4. Add the rest of the ingredients, including yogurt, and mix well.

5. This sauce can be used as a dip as well as a spread for pita bread.

CHAPTER 2

ISRAELI BEVERAGE RECIPES

ISRAELI CARDAMOM COFFEE

Serves: 2

Ingredients:
- 2 cups water
- 8 pods cardamom, powder the seeds
- 1 teaspoon grated ginger
- 1.4 ounces super-fine ground coffee
- ¼ teaspoon ground cinnamon or to taste
- Sugar to taste (optional)

Directions:
1. Add all the spices, sugar, coffee, and water into a copper pot or saucepan. Mix well. Do not stir after this.

2. Place the copper pot over low heat. When it nearly begins to boil, remove the pot from heat for 20-30 seconds. Place it back over heat.

3. Repeat the previous step 1-2 times.

4. Pour into cups and serve.

AUTHENTIC TURKISH COFFEE

Serves: 2

Ingredients:

- 2 cups water
- 2 pods cardamom, powder the seeds
- 2 tablespoons super-fine ground Turkish coffee
- Sugar to taste (optional)

Directions:

1. Add water and sugar into an ibrik pot or saucepan. Mix well.

2. Place the ibrik pot over low heat. When it begins to boil, remove the pot from heat.

3. Stir in cardamom and coffee. Place the pot back over heat. When foamy on top, turn off the heat.

4. Pour into cups and serve. Make sure that you put some foam of the coffee on top in each cup.

LIMONANA

Serves: 2

Ingredients:

- 2 lemons peeled, separate flesh from membranes, discard membranes, deseeded
- 4 teaspoons powdered sugar or to taste
- A handful fresh mint leaves
- 2 cups water
- Mint sprigs to garnish
- Ice cubes, as required

Directions:

1. Add lemon flesh, mint, and sugar into a blender. Pulse until the mint leaves are finely chopped.

2. Add water and pulse until well-combined.

3. Pour over ice cubes in glasses and serve garnished with mint sprigs.

ISRAELI SPIKED SACHLAV

Serves: 2

Ingredients:

For salep coconut milk:
- 2 cans full fat coconut milk
- 4 tablespoons salep (orchid root powder)

For cocktail:
- 6 ounces salep coconut milk
- 1 ounce raspberry liqueur
- 2 ounces nocello liqueur

For garnish:
- 1 tablespoon shaved coconut
- 1 tablespoon toasted, chopped pistachios
- 2 cinnamon sticks

Directions:

1. To make salep: Add salep and coconut milk into a blender and blend until well-combined. Use as much as required and store the rest in the refrigerator. Use about 3 ounces per serving.

2. To make cocktails: Add all the ingredients for the cocktail into the cocktail shaker and stir.

3. Using a milk frother, forth the mixture until frothy.

4. Divide into 2 mugs. Sprinkle coconut and pistachios on top. Lightly insert a cinnamon stick in each mug and serve.

TAHINI DATE SHAKE

Serves: 1

Ingredients:

- ½ cup milk of your choice
- 2 tablespoons tahini paste
- 2 drops vanilla extract
- 1 ripe banana, peeled, sliced
- 2 medjool dates, pitted, chopped
- ¼ teaspoon ground cinnamon or to taste
- Ice cubes, as required

Directions:

1. Place all the ingredients in a blender.

2. Blend until it gets to the right consistency.

3. Pour it into a glass. Serve right away.

RE-VIVE SHAKE

Serves: 2

Ingredients:

- 12 ounces vanilla yogurt, preferably frozen
- 6 ounces orange juice
- ¾ cup granola
- 12 frozen peach slices
- ¾ cup slivered almonds

Directions:

1. Toss everything in a blender and blend well, until it becomes frothy.

2. Pour in tall glasses and serve right away.

Naomi Hoffman

CHAPTER 3

ISRAELI BREAKFAST RECIPES

ISRAELI BREAKFAST SALAD

Serves: 2

Ingredients:

- 1 medium cucumber, peeled, halved lengthwise
- 1 cup crumbled feta cheese
- ½ green bell pepper, deseeded, finely chopped
- 2 tablespoons olive oil
- Salt to taste
- Black pepper, as per taste
- 2 tablespoons grated onion, drained
- ¼ cup cottage cheese
- 2 tablespoons lemon juice
- Fresh mint sprigs to garnish

Directions:

1. Prick the cucumber with a fork all over and season with salt. Set aside in a strainer for 30 minutes. Chop the cucumber into smaller pieces and add them into a bowl.

2. Add the remaining ingredients in another bowl and stir well. Set aside for a few minutes.

3. Add cucumber and mix well.

4. Garnish with mint sprigs.

5. Set aside for 30 minutes and serve.

CLASSIC SHAKSHUKA

Serves: 6

Ingredients:

- 3 medium yellow onions, thinly sliced
- 3 cloves garlic, sliced
- 3 bell peppers of different colors, deseeded, cut each into 8 slices
- ½ teaspoon sugar (optional)
- 6 eggs
- 3 tablespoons olive oil
- 1 ½ teaspoons ground cumin
- Salt to taste
- Freshly ground pepper to taste
- 6 ripe tomatoes, chopped

- ¾ teaspoon cayenne pepper flakes or thinly sliced red chili
- ½ cup water or as required
- Chopped fresh cilantro or parsley, for garnish

Directions:

1. Heat a heavy-bottomed pan over medium heat. When the pan heats, add cumin and stir for a few seconds until fragrant. Add oil and stir. Let it heat slightly.

2. Add onions and cook for a couple of minutes. Add bell peppers and cook for a couple of minutes.

3. Toss the garlic and cook until it becomes aromatic.

4. Add the tomatoes, salt, pepper, cayenne pepper, and sugar. Add a little water and stir. Cover and cook for about 15 minutes. Stir occasionally. The gravy should not be watery. It should be slightly on the thicker side.

5. Make 6 wells (cavities) at different spots in the gravy. Crack each egg, one at a time, and drop into each well. Cover with a fitting lid and cook until the eggs are cooked as per your preference.

6. Garnish with herbs and serve.

CHEESE BOUREKAS

Serves: 6

Ingredients:
- 1 large egg, beaten
- ½ teaspoon dried parsley
- 1/8 teaspoon onion powder
- 1/8 teaspoon garlic powder
- 1/8 teaspoon pepper
- ¼ teaspoon salt
- ½ package frozen (from a 17.5-ounce package) puff pastry
- 1 tablespoon sesame seeds
- 1 cup shredded mozzarella cheese
- 1 teaspoon water

To serve:
- Olives
- Salad
- Cheese
- Yogurt

Directions:
1. Divide the beaten egg into 2 bowls. Add cheese, parsley, onion powder, garlic powder, and salt into one of the bowls of beaten egg and whisk well.

2. Dust your countertop with some flour.

3. Place the puff pastry sheet on the countertop and cut into 6 square pieces.

4. Add a teaspoon of water to the other bowl of beaten egg. Beat well. This is the egg wash.

5. Brush lightly the edges of all the 6 pastry sheet squares with egg wash.

6. Divide the cheese filling among the squares and place in the center. Fold each in half, diagonally so that you get triangular shape bourekas.

7. Press the edges to seal. You can use a fork for sealing.

8. Place the bourekas on a greased baking sheet. Brush the top of the bourekas with egg wash.

9. Scatter sesame seeds on top.

10. Preheat the oven and bake at 350° F for about 25 minutes or until golden brown.

11. Take it out of the oven and let it cool.

12. Serve with a salad, olives, some cheese, and yogurt.

BAKED POLENTA WITH EGGS & ROASTED VEGETABLES

Serves: 2

Ingredients:

For polenta:

- 2 cups vegetable broth or water
- 1 teaspoon kosher salt
- ½ cup cornmeal
- 1 tablespoon extra-virgin olive oil
- Cooking spray

For roasted vegetables and eggs:

- 1 red pepper, diced
- 4 ounces mushrooms, sliced
- Extra-virgin olive oil, as required
- Freshly ground pepper to taste
- Salt to taste
- 4 eggs
- 3 scallions, sliced
- 1 cup halved grape tomatoes

For garnish:

- Hot sauce
- Za'atar
- Extra-virgin olive oil
- Hot sauce
- Sumac
- Matbucha

Directions:

1. To make polenta: Take a baking dish of about 6 inches and grease it well with cooking spray, on the bottom as well as the sides.

2. Add all the ingredients for polenta into the dish and stir until well-incorporated.

3. Bake in an oven at 350° F for about 30-40 minutes until cooked and soft. Before baking, make sure that you have preheated the oven. Stir every 12-13 minutes.

4. To make roasted vegetables: Meanwhile, place all the vegetables on a baking sheet lined with parchment paper.

5. Trickle oil over it. Sprinkle salt and pepper over the vegetables. Place the vegetables in the oven along with the polenta (about 5 minutes after the polenta is placed in the oven). The vegetables should be cooked in about 18-20 minutes.

6. Remove the baking sheet and crack eggs on top of the vegetables. Sprinkle salt and pepper over the eggs.

7. Place the baking sheet back in the oven and let the eggs cook; runny yolks and set whites taste great.

8. Take 2 bowls and add half the polenta into each bowl. Top with vegetables and eggs.

9. Garnish with the suggested garnishes and serve.

ISRAELI VEGAN POWER BOWL

Serves: 2

Ingredients:

- 1 small eggplant, cut into 1-inch cubes
- ½ red pepper, diced
- ½ red onion, thinly sliced
- 7-8 kale leaves, discards hard stems and ribs, chopped
- ¼ cup sliced almonds
- ½ teaspoon Ras al Hanout spice mix
- Freshly cracked pepper to taste
- 1 tablespoon hot water
- 1 cup cooked or canned chickpeas
- Extra-virgin olive oil, as required
- Salt to taste
- ¼ cup tahini
- ½ tablespoon lemon juice

For topping:

1. 1 small avocado, peeled, pitted, sliced
2. 1 cup halved grape tomatoes
3. 1 cup sliced cucumber

Directions:

1. Add all the vegetables, chickpeas, and almonds into a bowl. Drizzle oil. Season with salt pepper and Ras el Hanout and toss well.

2. Transfer the vegetable and chickpeas mixture onto a baking sheet. Spread out the mixture evenly.

3. Preheat your oven to 375° F before baking. Bake for about 30-40 minutes or until cooked and golden brown. Stir every 12-13 minutes.

4. Meanwhile, add lemon juice, tahini, hot water, and seasonings into a bowl and whisk well.

5. Take 2 bowls and add half the roasted vegetable mixture into each bowl.

6. Drizzle the tahini sauce on top. Top with suggested toppings and serve.

CHAPTER 4

ISRAELI SALADS AND SOUP RECIPES

CLASSIC ISRAELI SALAD

Serves: 3

Ingredients:

- 2 Persian cucumbers or 1 medium English cucumber, peel if desired, cut into ¼-inch cubes
- 2 scallions, trimmed, white and light green parts only, thinly sliced
- 1 medium red bell pepper, deseeded, cut into ¼-inch squares
- 2 medium tomatoes, deseeded, cut into ¼-inch squares
- 1 ½ tablespoons extra-virgin olive oil
- Salt to taste
- 1 ½ tablespoons fresh lemon juice
- Freshly ground pepper to taste

Directions:

1. Add all the vegetables, seasoning, lemon juice, and oil in a bowl and toss well.

2. Serve immediately.

ISRAELI COUSCOUS SALAD

Serves: 2

Ingredients:

- 1 cup Israeli couscous
- ½ veggie bouillon cube dissolved in a cup of water (broth)
- 5 Greek kalamata olives, diced
- ½ tablespoon olive oil
- 2 tablespoons diced red onions
- ¼ cucumber, diced

Directions:

1. Place a pot with oil and couscous over medium heat. Stir frequently until light brown.

2. Add broth and stir. When it starts boiling, lower the heat to low heat and cover with a lid. Cook until there is no more water left in the pot.

3. When done, fluff with a fork. Add couscous into a bowl and allow it to cool completely.

4. Add the rest of the ingredients and toss well.

5. Divide into bowls and serve.

LEMONY CUCUMBER COUSCOUS SALAD

Serves: 3

Ingredients:

- ¾ cup Israeli couscous
- 1 cup chopped parsley
- 1 tablespoon olive oil
- Salt to taste
- 1.5 ounces feta cheese, crumbled
- 1 medium cucumber
- Juice of ½ lemon
- A large pinch garlic powder
- Freshly cracked pepper to taste

Directions:

1. Cook the couscous and set aside to cool.

2. Add couscous, feta, cucumber, and parsley into a bowl and toss well.

3. Add oil, lemon juice, salt, pepper, and garlic powder into a bowl and toss well. Pour over the salad. Toss well. Chill if desired and serve.

TABBOULEH

Serves: 6-8

Ingredients:
- 10 scallions, chopped
- 1 ½-2 cups fine bulgur, soaked in hot water for 15 minutes, drained
- 4 cups chopped grape tomatoes
- Salt to taste
- 10-12 tablespoons olive oil
- 1 cup chopped, fresh mint
- 2 bunches fresh, flat-leaf parsley, chopped
- ½ cup fresh lemon juice or to taste
- 4 teaspoons ground cumin

Directions:
1. Let the drained bulgur remain in the strainer for 30-40 minutes. Transfer into a bowl.

2. Add lemon juice, olive oil, salt, cumin, and lemon and stir until well-combined. Cover and set aside for about 45 minutes for the flavors to blend in.

3. Add tomatoes, mint, and parsley into the bowl of bulgur and toss well. Pour dressing on top and toss well.

4. Garnish with some mint or parsley if desired and serve.

LEMON CHICKEN SOUP

Serves: 4

Ingredients:

- 5 cups chicken broth
- 4 cloves garlic, minced
- Zest of ½ large lemon
- ½ cup Israeli pearl couscous
- 1 ounce crumbled feta cheese
- 1 ½ tablespoons olive oil
- Salt to taste
- Pepper to taste
- ½ sweet onion, thinly sliced
- 1 boneless, skinless chicken breast
- ¼ teaspoon crushed red pepper
- 3 tablespoons chopped chives
- 3 large egg yolks, beaten
- Juice of a lemon

Directions:

1. Place a soup pot with oil, onion, and garlic over medium heat and sauté until onions are pink.

2. Mix in the broth, zest, chicken, and crushed red pepper.

3. When just starts boiling, lower the heat and let it simmer for 5-6 minutes.

4. Add couscous, pepper, and salt and stir. Cook for 5 minutes and remove from heat.

5. Using a pair of tongs, pull out the chicken from the pot, shred it with a pair of forks, and add it back into the pot.

6. Take out about ½ cup of the soup and pour it into the bowl of yolks, whisking simultaneously as you add.

7. Pour into the pot and keep whisking. Add feta, lemon juice, and chives and stir. Taste the soup and add some more seasonings if required.

8. Ladle into soup bowls and serve.

WHITE BEAN SOUP

Serves: 8

Ingredients:

For soup:

- 2 cups dry white or cannellini beans or 4 cans (15 ounces each) white or cannellini beans
- 2 tablespoons oil or as required
- 2 large onions, diced
- 2 carrots, diced
- 2 potatoes, diced
- 2 tomatoes, chopped
- 4 large bay leaves
- 20 cups chicken broth or vegetable broth
- Salt to taste
- Pepper to taste
- 2 large leeks, white part only, chopped
- 2 ribs celery, diced
- 12 cloves garlic, peeled
- Leaves from 6 sprigs thyme
- A handful fresh stems of parsley or cilantro, chopped
- Lemon juice to taste
- Zhug to taste

Directions:

1. If you want to use dried beans, soak in water overnight. Cook the beans and add 2 bay leaves and 8 cloves garlic while cooking.

2.   Place a large soup pot with oil, leeks, onion, celery, potatoes, and carrots and cook until tender.

3.   Add tomatoes, bay leaves, garlic, parsley stems, and thyme and stir fry for 2-3 minutes.

4.   Add broth, beans, salt, and pepper and mix well. Cover and cook on low heat for about 30 minutes.

5.   Remove from heat. Add lemon juice and stir.

6.   Ladle into soup bowls. Top with zhug and serve.

ISRAELI THICK LENTIL SOUP

Serves: 8

Ingredients:

- 2 cups dried lentils, rinsed well, soaked in water for a while
- 4 carrots, shredded
- 2 cups chopped onions
- 4 bay leaves
- Salt to taste or garlic salt to taste
- Pepper to taste
- ¼ cup chopped fresh parsley
- 1 teaspoon ground cumin
- 4 tablespoons lemon juice
- 4 cloves garlic, peeled, minced
- 6 cups chicken broth
- ½ teaspoon dried thyme
- 2 cups cooked, diced chicken or turkey
- 8 celery ribs, shredded
- 6 cups water
- ½ teaspoon turmeric powder or curry powder (optional)

Directions:

1. Set aside the chicken and lemon juice and add the remaining ingredients into a large soup pot.

2. Place the soup pot over high heat.

3. When the soup starts boiling, lower the heat to medium-low heat and cover the pot with a lid. Once the lentils are tender, turn off the heat.

4.   Add lemon juice and chicken and mix well. Heat thoroughly.

5.   Serve in soup bowls.

HAWAIJ LENTIL VEGETABLE SOUP

Serves: 4

Ingredients:

- 1 medium onion, diced
- 1 medium beet, diced
- 1 tablespoon hawaij spice
- 2 tablespoons tomato paste
- ½ teaspoon Himalayan salt
- 2 cups vegetable broth
- 2-3 carrots, diced
- 2 cloves garlic, minced
- 2 tablespoons olive oil
- ¼ cup pureed tomatoes
- 1 ½ cups lentils, rinsed, soaked in water overnight

Directions:

1. Place a soup pot over medium-high heat with a tablespoon of oil. When the oil is heated, add onions and cook until onions are slightly soft.

2. Add the carrots and cook for 5 minutes. Next, stir in the garlic and beets and cook for another 5 minutes.

3. Add hawaij spice mix and stir for about a minute. Stir in tomato paste and remaining oil.

4. Add pureed tomato, lentils, and salt and sauté for 5-6 minutes.

5. Stir in the broth. When the soup starts boiling, lower the heat to low heat and cook until lentils are tender.

6. Taste and adjust the seasoning if required.

7. Ladle into soup bowls and serve.

CHAPTER 5

ISRAELI MAIN COURSE RECIPES

ISRAELI CHICKEN SOFRITO

Serves: 4

Ingredients:
- 4 bone-in, skin-on chicken thighs
- 1 medium Russet potato, peeled cubed (1½-inch cubes)
- 1 medium yellow onion, sliced
- 2 small sweet potatoes, peeled, cubed (1½-inch cubes)
- 1 tablespoon extra-virgin olive oil
- Salt and freshly ground pepper to taste
- ¾ cup chicken stock
- ½ teaspoon turmeric powder
- 1 teaspoon paprika or to taste
- 2 bay leaves
- ¼ teaspoon garlic powder

Directions:
1. Place a Dutch oven or heavy pot over medium-high heat. Add oil and allow it to heat.

2. Meanwhile, sprinkle salt and a liberal amount of pepper over the chicken thighs.

3. Once the oil is heated, add chicken into the pot, with the skin side touching the bottom of the pot. Do not stir the chicken for about 6-8 minutes or until the skin of the chicken turns a darker shade of golden brown. Reduce the heat if desired while cooking.

4. Using tongs, take out the chicken from the pot and set aside.

5. Next add potatoes into the pot. Cook until golden brown all over. It need not be cooked through.

6. Using tongs, take out the potatoes from the pot and set aside.

7. Now add the sweet potatoes and cook until golden brown all over. It need not be cooked through.

8. Take out the sweet potatoes from the pot and set aside.

9. Next, add in the onions into the pot. Add a pinch of salt and mix well.

10. Lower the heat to medium and place a lid on the pot. Cook for 8-9 minutes. Stir occasionally.

11. Meanwhile, add chicken stock, spices, and bay leaves into a bowl and whisk well.

12. Remove the lid and cook until the onions are golden brown. Discard some of the cooked fat from the pot if desired.

13. Pour the stock mixture into the pot. Add chicken and stir. Scrape the pot to remove any particles that are stuck.

14. Cover the pot again and cook until chicken is cooked to the desired doneness.

15. Add potatoes and sweet potatoes and mix well.

16. Increase the heat to medium heat and cook until the potatoes are cooked through.

17. Add salt and pepper to suit your taste.

18. Serve hot.

CHICKEN SHAWARMA

Serves: 8 (2 stuffed pita halves)

Ingredients:

- ¼ cup finely chopped fresh parsley
- 1 teaspoon crushed red pepper
- ½ teaspoon cumin powder
- ½ teaspoon ground ginger
- ¼ teaspoon coriander powder
- 1 teaspoon salt
- 4 tablespoons fresh lemon juice, divided
- 2 pounds chicken breast halves, skinless, boneless, thinly sliced
- 2 tablespoons tahini
- 1/3 cup plain low-fat Greek-style yogurt, divided
- 6 garlic cloves, minced, divided

- ¼ cup extra-virgin olive oil
- 8 (6-inch each) pitas, halved
- 1 cup chopped plum tomato
- 1 cup chopped cucumber
- ½ cup chopped red onion

Directions:

1. Add salt, spices, parsley, 2 tablespoons yogurt, 2 tablespoons lemon juice, half the garlic, and ginger into a large bowl. Mix well.

2. Add chicken into the bowl. Stir to coat the chicken well.

3. Place a large nonstick skillet over medium heat. Add oil. Once the oil is hot, add chicken and cook until it becomes brown all over. It should be cooked inside as well.

4. Meanwhile, add the remaining yogurt, lemon juice, tahini, and garlic into a bowl and mix well. Smear the yogurt mixture inside the pita bread halves. Divide equally the chicken, cucumber, tomatoes, and onions among the pita halves.

5. Serve.

ISRAELI YELLOW CHICKEN & POTATOES

Serves: 4

Ingredients:

- 1 tablespoon oil
- 1 medium onion, chopped
- 2 chicken leg quarters, with skin and bone, cut
- 1 pound potatoes, cut into pieces lengthwise
- 1 teaspoon hawaij spice mix
- ½ teaspoon turmeric powder
- 1 teaspoon chicken bouillon powder
- Pepper to taste
- Salt to taste
- Water, as required

Directions:

1. Place a pan over medium heat. Add oil and allow it to heat. Place chicken in the pan, with the skin side facing down. Cook until golden brown.

2. Take out the chicken and place it on a plate.

3. Add onions into the pan and cook until light brown.

4. Stir in the potatoes and cook until light brown. Add the spices and stir until they become aromatic.

5. Add chicken and mix well. Cook for 50-60 seconds and add about a cup of water and stir.

6. Cover and cook on low heat until the chicken and potatoes are tender.

7. Season with salt and pepper.

8. Serve hot.

BAHARAT CHICKEN WITH LABNEH

Serves: 4

Ingredients:

For baharat chicken:
- 8 skin-on, boneless chicken thighs
- 1 teaspoon ground cinnamon
- 4 tablespoons baharat spice mix
- 2 tablespoons all-purpose flour
- Salt to taste
- Freshly ground pepper to taste
- 4 shallots, thinly sliced
- 6 tablespoons olive oil

To serve:
- Labneh, as required
- ½ cup pomegranate arils
- 2 baby gem lettuce, torn
- 4 flatbreads

Directions:

1. Add salt, pepper, cinnamon, and baharat spice mix into a bowl and stir well. Sprinkle this mixture all over the chicken. Keep it aside.

2. Place shallots in a bowl. Sprinkle flour over the shallots and toss well.

3. Place a large pan over medium-high heat. Add oil. Once hot, add half the shallots and fry until golden brown and crispy.

4. Take out the shallots and place them on a plate.

5. Add remaining shallots and cook until golden brown and crispy. Remove and place them on the plate. Turn off the heat.

6. Place a griddle pan over high heat. When the pan heats, place chicken, with the skin side facing down. Cook until it becomes brown on all sides. Turn off the heat.

7. Once cooked, place chicken on your cutting board. Cut into thick slices after it has cooled a bit.

8. To serve: Warm the flatbreads. Spread Labneh over the flatbreads. Place chicken slices over the flatbreads. Scatter lettuce leaves and pomegranate seeds on top and serve.

KOSHER ISRAELI CHICKEN SCHNITZEL

Serves: 2

Ingredients:

- 1 whole chicken breast, skinless, boneless, halved
- 1 egg, beaten
- Oil, to fry, as required
- Paprika to taste
- Salt to taste
- ¼ cup all-purpose flour
- ½ cup breadcrumbs
- ½ teaspoon garlic powder
- 1 teaspoon crushed, dried parsley

Directions:

1. Place flour on a plate.

2. Place breadcrumbs, salt, parsley, and spices in a shallow bowl and stir until well-combined.

3. Lay chicken breasts in between 2 plastic sheets on your work area. Pound the chicken using a meat mallet until it is about ¼-inch thick.

4. First dredge chicken in flour. Shake to drop off excess flour.

5. Next, dip them in egg. Shake to drop off extra egg.

6. Finally dredge in breadcrumbs. Shake to drop off excess breadcrumbs.

7. Place a pan over medium heat. Add 2-3 tablespoons of oil and let it heat. Add chicken in the pan and saute it until it becomes golden brown on one side. Repeat the same procedure for the other side until it becomes brown all over.

8. Remove from the pan and place it on paper towels so the excess oil is soaked.

9. Serve hot.

LAMB OSCO BUCCO

Serves: 2-3

Ingredients:

- 1 pound lamb slices, cut off the neck, bone-in, around 5 round slices
- ½ teaspoon salt
- 2 tablespoons olive oil or more if required
- ¼ cup diced celery
- ½ onion, chopped
- 1 carrot, diced
- 1 bay leaf
- 3 cloves garlic, peeled, sliced
- ½ cup dry red wine
- 1 tomato, chopped
- ½ cup flour
- ¼ teaspoon pepper
- 1 cup chicken stock

Directions:

1. Place flour on a plate. Add salt and pepper and mix well.

2. Dredge lamb slices in flour. Shake to drop off excess flour.

3. Place a skillet with oil over medium heat. Once hot, place lamb slices and cook until golden brown all over.

4. Transfer onto a plate.

5. Add some more oil if necessary. Add bay leaf, onion, celery, and carrot and stir. Cook until slightly tender.

6. Stir in the garlic. Cook for 50-60 seconds or until it gets aromatic.

7. Increase the heat to high heat. Add red wine. Scrape the pan to remove any stuck particles.

8. Cook until nearly dry. Add lamb and tomatoes and mix well.

9. Add broth and stir. Turn off the heat.

10. Transfer into a baking dish.

11. Place the baking dish in a preheated oven and bake at 350° F for about 80-90 minutes until it gets aromatic.

12. A serving of steamed greens pairs up well with this dish.

LEMONY HUMMUS KAWARMA

Serves: 3

Ingredients:

For kawarma:
- 6 ounces neck fillet of lamb, finely chopped
- ½ teaspoon ground allspice
- 1/8 teaspoon freshly ground black pepper
- 1/8 teaspoon freshly ground white pepper
- ¼ teaspoon ground cinnamon
- 1/8 teaspoon freshly grated nutmeg
- ½ teaspoon za'atar spice mix
- ½ tablespoon chopped mint
- ½ tablespoon chopped, flat-leaf parsley
- ½ teaspoon olive oil
- ½ teaspoon salt
- ½ tablespoon unsalted butter or ghee

For lemon sauce:
- 2 tablespoon fresh lemon juice
- 1 tablespoon finely chopped flat-leaf parsley
- ½ green chili, finely chopped
- 1 clove garlic, crushed
- 1 tablespoon white wine vinegar
- Salt to taste

To garnish:

- 1 tablespoon toasted pine nuts
- 1 tablespoon chopped, flat leaf parsley
- Cooked or canned chickpeas
- Hummus, as required

Directions:

1. For kawarma: Set aside butter and oil and add the remaining ingredients in a bowl.

2. Stir until well-combined. Cover and chill for 30 minutes.

3. Just before you cook meat, make the lemon sauce as follows: Add all the ingredients for lemon sauce into a bowl and whisk well.

4. Place a large pan over medium-high heat. Add butter and oil. When butter melts, add meat and sauté for a couple of minutes, no longer than this. Turn off the heat.

5. Take 3 shallow bowls. Place 4-5 tablespoons of hummus in each bowl. Make a cavity in the center of the hummus. Divide the kawarma among the cavities.

6. Scatter chickpeas, parsley and pine nuts on top.

7. Spoon lemon sauce on top and serve.

BAHARAT LAMB

Serves: 8 (3 per serving)

Ingredients:

- 24 lamb cutlets
- 4 tablespoons olive oil
- 4-5 tablespoons baharat spice mix

To serve:

- Tabouli
- Lebanese bread
- Tzatziki

Directions:

1. Add oil and baharat spice mix into a bowl and mix well. Smear this mixture all over the lamb cutlets.

2. Place the cutlets on a plate. Cover and chill for 30-45 minutes.

3. Preheat a grill pan. Place the lamb cutlets (in batches) on the pan and cook for 3 minutes. Turn the cutlets and cook for 3 minutes or to the desired doneness.

4. Serve with suggested serving options.

ISRAELI LAMB STEW WITH DILL & OLIVES

Serves: 3

Ingredients:

- ¼ cup extra-virgin olive oil
- 1 onion, finely chopped
- Salt to taste
- 1 ½ pounds lamb shoulder or stew meat, cut into 2-inch cubes
- ½ teaspoon turmeric powder
- ½ cup beef stock
- ¾ pound spinach, chopped
- 4 green onions, white part only, finely chopped
- 1 cup peeled, diced, boiled potatoes
- Freshly ground pepper to taste
- 6 tablespoons lemon juice
- 1 bunch celery, use only leaves, finely chopped
- 1 tablespoon minced fresh dill
- ½ cup pitted, halved, green olives

Directions:

1. Place a heatproof casserole dish over medium heat, with a tablespoon of oil. Once hot, add onions and meat and cook until brown, stirring occasionally.

2. Mix in the salt, pepper, and turmeric.

3. Stir in stock and lemon juice. Mix well.

4. Lower the heat and cook for 10-12 minutes. Stir often.

5. Add celery, spinach and green onions into a heavy-bottomed skillet. Cook until they wilt.

6. Add 3 tablespoons of oil and cook for 3-4 minutes. Transfer into the casserole dish and mix well.

7. Add potatoes, olives, and dill and mix well. Cover and cook until tender. Stir frequently.

8. Serve with bread or over rice or couscous.

BEEF SHAKSHUKA WITH SMOKED EGGPLANT

Serves: 2

Ingredients:

- 2 eggplants (about 1.2 pounds in all)
- ½ large onion, finely chopped
- ¼ teaspoon ground cumin
- ¼ teaspoon chili flakes
- ¼ teaspoon ground cumin
- ½ teaspoon sumac
- 5.3 ounces beef mince
- 3 cloves garlic, chopped
- Pepper to taste
- Salt to taste
- 1 tomato, chopped
- ½ tablespoon tomato paste
- 2-3 tablespoons water
- 2 teaspoons chopped parsley
- 1 ½ teaspoons olive oil + extra to drizzle
- 2 eggs
- 1 teaspoon finely chopped preserved lemon
- Tahini sauce to serve

Directions:

1. Prick the eggplant all over with a fork. Put on your gas heat and place the eggplant over the heat and cook until charred outside and cooked inside. Turn the eggplant frequently.

2. Place a heavy-bottomed pan with oil over medium-high heat. Once hot, add onion, garlic, and spices and cook until onions are soft.

3. You can now add in the beef, tomato paste, and salt. Mix well. Raise the heat to high heat. Cook until the meat is brown.

4. Meanwhile, peel the eggplant and mash it lightly.

5. Add eggplant, tomato, and preserved lemon and mix well. Sauté for 2-4 minutes.

6. Add water and mix well. Make 2 holes in the mixture. Crack an egg into each hole. Place a lid on the pan and cook until the yolks are barely cooked and the whites are cooked.

7. Turn off the heat. Garnish with sumac and parsley. Drizzle some oil on top. Drizzle tahini sauce on top and serve right away.

SALMON WITH SOUR CREAM & ZA'ATAR

Serves: 2

Ingredients:
- ¾ pound salmon, skinless, cut into 2 equal pieces
- Freshly ground pepper to taste
- 2 tablespoons fat-free sour cream or soy sour cream
- ½ teaspoon coarse salt
- ½ tablespoon canola oil or grapeseed oil
- ½ tablespoon za'atar spice mix

Directions:
1. Place a heavy skillet over medium heat. Let the pan heat well.

2. Add oil and let it heat as well.

3. Season salmon (on one side) with half the salt and some pepper and place it in the pan, with the salted side facing down.

4. Season the other side with remaining salt and some pepper.

5. Cook until it becomes golden brown and crisp on one side. Flip sides and cook on medium-low heat and cook until the fish is cooked to the desired level of doneness.

6. Remove the fish and place on individual serving plates. Drizzle sour cream on the fish. Sprinkle za'atar spice mix on top and serve.

ISRAELI SEAFOOD PAELLA

Serves: serves 12-15

For croutons:
- 6 slices og day old, sourdough bread or challah bread or flatbread, torn or cut into cubes
- 4 tablespoons olive oil
- 2 tablespoons za'atar spice mix

For marinated za'atar:
- 2 small red onions, thinly sliced
- 4 tablespoons sumac
- 4 tablespoons olive oil
- 4 bunches fresh oregano or thyme, use only the leaves
- Juice of a lemon
- 1 teaspoon sea salt

For stewed tomatoes:
- 11 pounds multi-colored cherry tomatoes, quartered
- 6 tablespoons olive oil
- 2 teaspoons pepper or to taste
- 8 cloves garlic, peeled
- 2 tablespoons sea salt

For seafood:
- 24 jumbo shrimp or prawns, peeled, deveined
- 40 calamari, cleaned
- 7 ounces feta cheese, crumbled
- Olive oil, as required

To serve:
- Lime wedges
- Sumac
- Fresh thyme leaves, chopped

Directions:

1. To make croutons: Add bread into a bowl. Sprinkle za'atar spice mix and olive oil over it. Toss well and spread on a baking sheet that is lined with parchment paper.

2. Bake in a preheated oven at 400° F for about 15 minutes or until crisp and brown on the outside.

3. Take out the baking sheet and let it cool completely. Transfer into an airtight container until use.

4. For marinated za'atar: Add all the ingredients for marinated za'atar into a bowl and mix well. Set aside to marinate for 20-30 minutes.

5. To make stewed tomatoes: Add all the ingredients for stewed tomatoes into a large bowl and toss well. Transfer onto 2 baking sheets that are lined with parchment paper.

6. Preheat an oven to 500° F and grill for about 20 minutes or until slightly soft. Roast in batches.

7. Place a grill pan over medium heat. When the pan is heated, spray some cooking spray.

8. Cook the calamari and prawns for 1-2 minutes on each side. Cook in batches.

9. Serve on individual serving plates in this manner: Spread some stewed tomatoes on the plate. Place a layer of seafood and croutons. Sprinkle some feta cheese. Next, spoon some marinated za'atar followed by sumac and fresh thyme leaves. Serve with lemon wedges.

SABICH SANDWICHES (PITAS WITH EGGPLANT, EGGS, HUMMUS, AND TAHINI)

Serves: 8

Ingredients:

- 1 cup tahini sauce
- 1 ½ cups hummus
- ½ head cabbage, thinly shredded
- 14 ounces plum tomatoes, diced
- 1 ½ pounds Italian eggplant, cut into ½-inch thick round slices
- 1 large seedless cucumber, diced
- 2 tablespoons minced, flat-leaf parsley
- 4 tablespoons white wine vinegar
- Olive oil, to fry, as required
- Kosher salt to taste
- 4 tablespoons fresh lemon juice

To serve:

- 8 hard-boiled eggs, peeled, sliced
- 8 fresh round pita bread, warmed, split slightly to make a pocket
- Israeli pickles, as required
- Amba, as required

Directions:

1. Sprinkle salt over the tomatoes and place them in a fine wire mesh strainer. Place the strainer over a bowl to collect the drippings, which is to be discarded. Let it remain this way for 30 minutes.

2. Place a large skillet over medium-high heat. Add enough oil in the pan so that it is ¼-inch from the bottom of the pan. Let the oil heat.

3. When the oil is well heated but not smoking, add eggplant slices in batches and cook until golden brown all over. Stir occasionally.

4. Remove and place on a baking sheet lined.

5. Season with salt. Set aside.

6. Add tomatoes, cucumber, parsley, and lemon juice into a bowl and toss well add a pinch of salt and toss well.

7. Place cabbage in a bowl. Add vinegar and a little salt and toss well.

8. Spread about 3 tablespoons of hummus inside each pita pocket. Place a few fried eggplant slices inside each pita pocket. Spoon some tahini sauce. Place egg slices and Israeli pickles. Spoon some more tahini sauce.

9. Next, spread some tomato salad in each pita. Finally, spoon amba and serve right away.

ISRAELI COUSCOUS & ZA'ATAR WITH TOMATO-BRAISED OKRA

Serves: 4

Ingredients:

- 2 tablespoons tomato paste
- 3 tablespoons extra-virgin olive oil
- 2 cans (14.1 ounces each) chopped tomatoes
- Salt to taste
- Pepper to taste
- 6 cloves garlic, finely sliced
- 2 red onions, chopped
- 3 tablespoons za'atar spice mix
- 28.2 ounces okra, trimmed
- Zest of 2 lemons, finely grated
- Juice of 2 lemons

To serve:

- Israeli couscous
- Greek yogurt
- A handful fresh dill, chopped
- Za'atar spice mix

Directions:

1. Place a pan over high heat and add oil. Once the oil is hot, saute the onions and garlic for about 3 minutes.

2. Stir in za'atar until it turns aromatic.

3. Now, stir in the tomato paste and cook for a minute.

4. It is now time to add the okra, lemon zest, tomatoes, and salt and pepper. Mix everything well.

5. Reduce the heat and put a lid on it. Cook until okra is tender. Do not overcook.

6. Stir in lemon juice and some of the dill. Add more lemon juice, salt, and pepper to taste if desired.

7. Serve Israeli couscous (recipe is given in the side dish chapter) in bowls.

8. Top with okra along with the cooked sauce. Sprinkle dill and za'atar and serve along with yogurt.

HERB & GINGER FISHCAKES WITH BEETROOT RELISH

Serves: 2

Ingredients:

For fishcakes:

- 2 firm white fish fillets, skinless, boneless, finely chopped
- A handful mint leaves, chopped
- A handful dill, chopped
- 1 teaspoon chopped tarragon
- Zest of ½ lemon, grated
- 1 teaspoon finely grated ginger
- 2 small cloves garlic, crushed
- ¼ teaspoon ground turmeric
- ½ teaspoon ground cumin
- ¾ teaspoon salt
- 1 egg
- ¼ cup breadcrumbs
- Pepper to taste
- 1 teaspoon sunflower oil
- 4 mild, long green peppers

For beetroot relish:

- 5.3 ounces cooked beetroots, finely grated
- A large pinch ground cumin
- A large pinch caster sugar
- ¾ tablespoon olive oil
- Pepper to taste
- 2 tablespoons sour cream

- 1 ½ teaspoons white wine vinegar
- 2 tablespoons freshly grated horseradish
- ¼ teaspoon salt

Directions:

1. To make beetroot relish: Place grated beetroot in a colander for about 20 minutes.

2. Add beetroot, cumin, sugar, oil, pepper, sour cream, vinegar, horseradish, and salt into a bowl and stir until well-combined. Cover and set aside for a while for the flavors to blend in.

3. Keep aside the oil and green pepper and add the remaining ingredients for fish cakes into a bowl and mix well.

4. Make into 4-6 equal portions of the mixture and shape into patties.

5. Place an ovenproof skillet over. When the pan is well heated, add green chili and cook until blisters appear on them. Take out the chilies and place them on a plate.

6. Clean the pan and place it back over heat. Add oil and let it heat. Add fishcakes and cook until the underside is light brown.

7. Turn the fishcakes and cook the other side until it becomes light brown. Turn off the heat.

8. Now place the skillet in a preheated oven.

9. Bake at 350° F for about 8 minutes until well-cooked inside.

10. Divide the fishcakes and peppers among 2 plates. Serve with beetroot relish.

ISRAELI RICE & LENTIL STEW

Serves: 3

Ingredients:

- ½ cup dried lentils, rinsed, soaked in water for 30 minutes
- 1 ½ tablespoons vegetable oil
- 2 cloves garlic, chopped
- 1 cup vegetable broth or water
- 1 large onion, chopped
- Freshly ground pepper to taste
- Salt to taste
- ½ teaspoon ground cumin
- ¾ cup long grain rice
- 1 ½ cups water
- A handful fresh parsley, chopped

Directions:

1. Add broth and lentils into a saucepan or pot. Place the saucepan over medium heat.

2. When it starts boiling, cook covered on low heat until tender. Turn off the heat.

3. Pour water into the pot of lentils.

4. Place a skillet with oil over medium heat. As the oil heats, add onions and cook until brown.

5. Stir in the cumin and garlic and cook for a few seconds until it gets aromatic. Turn off the heat.

6. Place the pot of lentils back over heat. When it begins to boil, add the rice and salt and stir.

7. Place a lid on the pot and cook on low until tender. Do not stir.

8. Remove the saucepan from heat. Using a fork, fluff the rice.

9. Add seasonings to taste. Stir in parsley and serve.

CLASSIC VEGAN FALAFEL

Serves: 8-9

Ingredients:

- ¼ cup chopped fresh parsley
- ¼ cup chopped fresh cilantro
- Olive oil to fry
- ½-¾ cup flour
- 1 large white onion, chopped
- 1 cup dried chickpeas, soaked in water overnight
- ¾ teaspoon salt or to taste
- ½ teaspoon red pepper flakes
- 2 teaspoons baking powder
- ½ teaspoon ground coriander
- ½ tablespoon ground cumin
- 8 cloves garlic, minced
- Cayenne pepper to taste
- 2 teaspoons salt

To serve:

- Tahini sauce (optional)
- Chopped tomatoes
- Diced onions
- Hummus (optional)
- Pita bread or lettuce
- Pickled turnips

Directions:

1. Drain the water from the chickpeas and lay them on kitchen towels so that the excess moisture is soaked out.

2. Add onion, parsley, cilantro, and garlic into the food processor bowl. Process until roughly chopped.

3. Add chickpeas, spices, and salt and process until very finely chopped but not mushy.

4. Sprinkle flour and baking powder and give short pulses for a few seconds until just incorporated.

5. Add the mixture in a bowl and cover with a lid. Refrigerate for 4-6 hours.

6. Divide the mixture into 8-9 equal portions and shape into patties or balls.

7. Place a deep pan over medium-high heat. Pour enough oil to cover the pan by about 3 inches in height.

8. Let the oil heat at about 375° F, then place a few falafels in the pan. Cook the falafels until golden brown all over. Remove and set aside.

9. Cook the remaining falafels in a similar manner.

10. Serve in pita bread or over lettuce leaves tahini sauce or hummus. It tastes good by itself too, as an appetizer with tahini sauce or hummus as dip.

ISRAELI BEANS WITH RICE

Serves: 3

Ingredients:

For soaking beans:
- 1 ½ cups navy beans
- ½ tablespoon salt
- 2 cups water

Other ingredients:
- 1 ½ tablespoons olive oil
- 2 cloves garlic, minced
- 1 tablespoon paprika
- ½-1 tablespoon white sugar
- 4 ¼ cups water
- ½ large onion, sliced
- 1-2 tablespoons tomato paste
- 1 tablespoon vegetarian chicken bouillon powder
- 1 teaspoon ground cumin
- A pinch baking soda
- Hot cooked rice to serve

Directions:

1. Soak beans in water with salt overnight. Discard any beans that rise on top the next day.

2. Drain off the soaked water.

3. Heat a pressure cooker or instant pot. Add oil. When the oil is heated, add onions and cook until brown.

4. Stir in tomato paste, vegetarian bouillon powder, cumin, paprika, and sugar and stir well.

5. Next, add in the drained beans, water, salt, and baking soda. Cover the pressure cooker and cook for about 30 minutes or until cooked.

6. If it is very thick, add some more water.

7. Serve over hot cooked rice.

HAWAIJ COUSCOUS

Serves: 6-8

Ingredients:

- 6 tablespoons olive oil, divided
- 12 ounces button mushrooms, sliced
- 3 bags (8.8 ounces each) Israeli couscous
- Kosher salt to taste
- 1 ½ large onions, diced
- 3 heaping tablespoons hawaij spice mix
- 1 ½ cans (15 ounces each) chickpeas, rinsed, drained
- 7 ½ cups water

Directions:

1. Place a large deep skillet over medium heat. Add 3 tablespoons of oil. Once the oil is hot, add onions and saute for 3 minutes.

2. Stir in the mushrooms and cook until brown.

3. Stir in the rest of the oil and hawaij spice and stir for a few seconds.

4. Stir in the couscous and let it toast lightly.

5. Stir in the chickpeas and water. Raise the heat to high. Let it cook this way until it boils. Now cover with a lid and cook on low until dry.

6. Fluff with a fork and serve.

CHAPTER 6

ISRAELI SIDE DISH RECIPES

ISRAELI PITA BREAD (PILOT)

Serves: 5 (2 pita breads per serving)

Ingredients:

- 2 cups all-purpose flour
- 1 package (¼ ounce) active dry yeast
- ½ teaspoon sea salt
- ¾ cup lukewarm water
- ½ teaspoon sugar

Directions:

1. Add lukewarm water, sugar, and yeast into a mixing bowl. Stir and set aside in a warm area until frothy. It should take around 10 minutes.

2. Mix together flour and salt in another bowl and stir. Add into the bowl of yeast and mix until dough is formed.

3. Dust your countertop with some flour. Place the dough on the countertop and knead the dough for a few minutes until supple.

4. Keep the dough in a greased bowl. Cover with cling wrap and place in a warm place until it doubles in size. It may take an hour.

5. Hit the dough a few times with your fist. Divide the dough into 10 equal portions and shape into balls.

6. Place a sheet of parchment paper on a large baking sheet. Use 2 baking sheets if desired.

7. Dust your countertop with some flour. Place a ball of dough on it and roll it into a thin round. Place it on a baking sheet lined with parchment paper. Use 2 baking sheets if desired.

8. Repeat with the remaining balls of dough. Leave some gap between each of the pita rounds on the baking sheet.

9. Place rack in the bottom of the oven.

10. Place the baking sheet in a preheated oven. Bake at 350° F for about 5-7 minutes. Watch the pita breads after about 5 minutes of baking time as they can get burnt.

11. Take out the baking sheet from the oven and set aside to cool for a few minutes.

12. You can serve it with hummus, falafel, shawarma, baba ganoush, etc. You can also fill some salad in the pitas and serve.

ISRAELI EGGPLANT & RED PEPPER SALAD

Serves: 4-5

Ingredients:

- 1 ½-2 pounds eggplants, trimmed, cut into ½-inch thick slices
- 1 red bell pepper, cored, cut into strips
- 1 tablespoon white wine vinegar
- Sea salt to taste
- Canola oil, as required
- 3 tablespoons ketchup
- 2 cloves garlic, peeled, smashed, finely chopped
- 1 tablespoon chopped parsley (optional)

Directions:

1. Sprinkle salt over the eggplant slices and place in a colander. Place the colander over a bowl. Let the moisture drain for 30 minutes.

2. Rinse the eggplant slices under running water. Drain well. Dry the slices with paper towels.

3. Place a wok or deep pan over medium-high heat. Pour enough oil (3-4 cups) into the pan.

4. When the oil is well heated and not smoking, about 375° F, add a few eggplant slices.

5. Cook until golden brown, turning occasionally. Remove them and place them on a plate.

6. Fry the remaining eggplant slices similarly.

7. Retain a little of the oil in the pan and take out the rest. Add red pepper slices into the pan and stir-fry for 3-5 minutes, until slightly tender.

8. Add eggplant and red pepper into a bowl.

9. Whisk together ketchup, vinegar, and garlic into a bowl. Add into the bowl of eggplant and stir lightly.

10. Cover the bowl with a lid and chill for 6-8 hours.

11. Garnish with parsley and serve.

ISRAELI COUSCOUS

Serves: 2-3

Ingredients:

- ½ tablespoon olive oil
- 2 tablespoons pistachios
- 2 tablespoons pine nuts
- 1 tablespoon barberries (optional)
- 1 medium onion, very thinly sliced
- 2 inches cinnamon stick
- 2 tablespoons raisins
- Zest of ½ lemon, grated
- 1 cup pearl couscous
- 1 tablespoon butter
- Salt to taste
- 1 ¼ cups chicken broth

Directions:

1. Place a deep skillet with oil over medium-high heat. Once hot, add the nuts and cook until lightly toasted.

2. Remove and place on a plate.

3. Next, add butter into the same skillet. Once butter melts, add onions, cinnamon, and couscous. Stir-fry until light brown.

4. Stir in broth. Once it starts boiling, cook on low heat until tender.

5. Turn off the heat.

6. Add the remaining ingredients and mix well.

7. Serve hot.

ISRAELI RICE PILAF

Serves: 4

Ingredients:

- 1 ¼ ounces vermicelli noodles, break into 1½-inch pieces
- 1 cup basmati rice
- ½ teaspoon sea salt
- 2 tablespoons pine nuts
- 2 tablespoons olive oil
- 2 cups chicken stock or broth
- ½ onion, chopped
- 2 tablespoons currants or sultanas

Directions:

1. Place a nonstick pan over medium heat. Add half the oil and let it heat. Once hot, add vermicelli noodles and stir-fry until brown. Be very careful while frying as it can get burnt.

2. Add in the rice and stir fry for a couple of minutes or until rice turns translucent.

3. Stir in the salt and stock and let it come to a boil.

4. After a few minutes, place a lid on the pan. Cook on low heat until dry.

5. Meanwhile, place a small pan over medium heat. Add 1 tablespoon oil. When the oil is heated, add onions and saute until it turns brown.

6. Stir in the pine nuts and currants and stir frequently until toasted lightly. Turn off the heat.

7. Spoon the rice into a serving bowl.

8. Garnish with caramelized onion mixture and serve.

ISRAELI YELLOW RICE

Serves: 6

Ingredients:

- 2 cups rice
- 1 teaspoon turmeric powder
- 4 teaspoons vegetarian or chicken bouillon powder
- 4 tablespoons oil
- 4 cups boiling water
- ½ teaspoon pepper

Directions:

1. Add oil into a pot and place over medium heat. Swirl the pot so that the oil spreads.

2. Let the oil heat. Add rice and stir-fry for a few minutes until rice turns opaque.

3. Add pepper and turmeric and mix well. Stir for about 10-15 seconds.

4. Add turmeric, bouillon powder, and water and bring to a boil. Simmer on low heat until dry.

5. Remove the pot from heat. Loosen the rice with a fork.

6. Serve hot.

ISRAELI GREEN RICE

Serves: 3

Ingredients:

- 1 tablespoon extra-virgin olive oil
- 2 cloves garlic, peeled, minced
- 1 cup chopped, fresh, mixed herbs (use a mixture of parsley, basil, dill, mint and tarragon)
- Freshly ground pepper to taste
- Kosher salt to taste
- 1 shallot, thinly sliced
- ¾ cup basmati rice, rinsed well
- 1 ½ cups boiling water

Directions:

1. Place a saucepan over medium-high heat. Add oil. Once the oil becomes hot, add shallots and garlic and cook for 3-4 minutes.

2. Add the rice and stir-fry for a few minutes until the rice turns translucent.

3. Pour water and stir. Cover and cook until water and rice are even. Remove from heat. Do not uncover for 10-15 minutes.

4. Add herbs and fluff with a fork, mixing the herbs in the rice.

5. Serve hot.

ROASTED SWEET POTATOES & FRESH FIGS

Serves: 3

Ingredients:

- 1.1 pounds small sweet potatoes, unpeeled, halved lengthwise, cut into wedges
- 1½ tablespoons balsamic vinegar
- 6 green onions, halved lengthwise, cut into 1½-inch pieces
- 3 ripe figs
- Sea salt to taste
- Freshly ground pepper to taste
- 2 ½ tablespoons olive oil
- ¾ tablespoon very fine sugar
- ½ red chili, thinly sliced
- 2.5 ounces soft goat's milk cheese (optional)

Directions:

1. Add 1½ tablespoons of oil, pepper and about a teaspoon of salt into a bowl and stir.

2. Add potato wedges and stir until well coated. Transfer onto a baking sheet. Place them with the cut side facing up.

3. Roast in a preheated oven at 475° F for about 20-30 minutes or until fork-tender.

4. Meanwhile, add sugar and vinegar in a small pan. Heat the pan on medium heat and the cook contents until they become slightly thick. Turn off the heat and let it cool. Add a few drops of water if it becomes too thick.

5. Take out the baking sheet and let it cool.

6. Place a pan over medium heat and Add 1 tablespoon oil. Once the oil gets hot, add green onions and chili and cook until slightly soft. Turn off the heat.

7. Transfer the sweet potatoes onto a serving platter. Spread the green onion mixture over the sweet potatoes. Chop the figs and place over the sweet potatoes. Spoon the balsamic reduction on top. Scatter goat cheese on top and serve.

CHAPTER 7

ISRAELI APPETIZER AND

SNACK RECIPES

KETZITZOT WITH TAHINA

Serves: 15-20

Ingredients:

For meatballs:
- 3 pounds ground turkey or beef
- 2 teaspoons sumac
- 2 large eggs
- Salt to taste
- Pepper to taste
- 2 onions, grated
- 2 teaspoons ground cumin

- 8 large cloves garlic, peeled, minced
- 2 cups chopped parsley
- 6-8 tablespoons breadcrumbs
- Olive oil, to fry, as required

To serve:
- Tahini sauce, for drizzle

Directions:
1. Set aside the oil and add the remaining ingredients in a bowl and incorporate well.

2. Make oval-shaped meatballs.

3. Place a large pan over high heat. Heat 2-3 tablespoons of oil. Fry a few meatballs in the pan. Do not overcrowd the pan. Cook until golden brown all over.

4. Remove and place it on a plate.

5. Repeat steps 3-4 and fry the remaining meatballs.

6. Transfer the meatballs onto a large serving platter. Drizzle tahini sauce on top of the meatballs and serve.

PITA CHIPS

Serves: 12-15

Ingredients:

- 6 pita breads, cut each into 8 triangles
- ¼ teaspoon black pepper
- ¼ teaspoon dried basil
- ¼ cup olive oil
- ½ teaspoon garlic salt
- ½ teaspoon dried chervil

Directions:

1. Spread the pita pieces on a baking sheet lined with parchment paper.

2. Add pepper, basil, oil, garlic salt, and chervil into a bowl and stir. Brush this mixture on the triangles.

3. Place in a preheated oven and bake at 400° F for about 7-9 minutes or until light brown and crisp. Keep a watch over the chips after about 6-7 minutes of baking as it can get burnt.

EGGPLANT VEGETARIAN CHOPPED LIVER

Serves: 5-6

Ingredients:
- 1 large eggplant, cut into ½-inch slices
- Olive oil, to fry
- 1 large clove garlic, peeled, chopped
- ½ teaspoon salt or to taste
- 1/3 cup flour
- ½ large onion, chopped
- 2 hard-boiled eggs, shelled, chopped
- Pepper to taste

Directions:
1. Sprinkle salt over the eggplant slices and place in a colander. Place the colander over a bowl. Let the moisture drain for 30 minutes.

2. Rinse the eggplant slices under running water. Drain well. Dry the slices with paper towels.

3. Dust the eggplant slices with flour, on either side.

4. Place a large pan over medium-high heat. Pour enough oil into the pan so that the bottom of the pan is coated with oil.

5. When the oil is well heated, add a few eggplant slices.

6. Cook until golden brown. Remove and place on a plate.

7.   Fry the remaining eggplant slices similarly, adding more oil if required.

8.   When all the eggplant slices are fried, add garlic and onion into the same pan. Cook until onion turns light golden brown. Stir occasionally. Turn off the heat.

9.   Transfer into the food processor bowl along with eggs and pulse until smooth. Add salt and pepper and pulse again.

10. Store in the refrigerator. Chill for a few hours and serve.

MUHAMMARA

Serves: 4

Ingredients:

- ½ jar roasted red peppers, drained (from a 12 ounces jar)
- 3 tablespoons breadcrumbs
- ½-2/3 cup walnuts
- 1 tablespoon extra-virgin olive oil
- ½ teaspoon paprika
- 1 large clove garlic, peeled,
- ½ teaspoon fresh lemon juice
- ½ teaspoon ground cumin
- ¼ teaspoon cayenne pepper or ½ teaspoon Aleppo pepper
- Salt to taste

To serve:
- Pita chips
- Chopped parsley or mint leaves
- Olive oil, to drizzle (optional)

Directions:

1. Gather all the ingredients and add them into the food processor bowl. Process until rough in texture.

2. Pour into a bowl. Sprinkle parsley on top. Trickle olive oil on top if using and serve along with pita chips.

PICKLED CAULIFLOWER

Serves: 8

Ingredients:

- 6 tablespoons coriander seeds
- 1 teaspoon white mustard seeds
- 1 teaspoon celery seeds (optional)
- 2 teaspoons turmeric powder
- 1 teaspoon cumin seeds
- 6 bay leaves
- 2 large carrots, chopped into chunks
- 2 heads cauliflower, cut into florets
- 1 small yellow onion, sliced
- 6 tablespoons sugar
- Cayenne pepper to taste
- 4 teaspoon kosher salt
- Water, as required

Directions:

1. Fill a large saucepan (up to ¾) with water and heat on high heat.

2. Once it starts boiling, add carrots and cauliflower and let it boil for 3 minutes. Drain off the water and add the vegetables into a large bowl.

3. Combine all the spices in a bowl.

4. Add half the spice mixture into a large container (with lid). You can use a large glass jar as well. Place carrots and cauliflower over the spices.

5. Add 4 cups of water, salt, and sugar in a pan and place it over medium-high heat. Bring to a boil, stirring frequently. When sugar dissolves completely, turn off the heat. Add vinegar and stir.

6. Pour over the vegetables. Sprinkle remaining spices on top. Fasten the lid and refrigerate for 24-48 hours.

7. Serve.

KIBBEH

Serves: 12-16

Ingredients:

For shell:
- 2 ½ cups fine bulgur
- 2 teaspoons kosher salt or to taste
- 1 teaspoon ground coriander
- 2 teaspoons ground cumin
- Freshly ground pepper to taste
- 2 pounds ground lamb
- 1 large yellow onion, finely chopped

For filling:
- 4 tablespoons extra-virgin olive oil
- 2 large yellow onions, finely chopped
- 4 teaspoons ground allspice
- 4 teaspoons ground cinnamon
- 2/3 cup pine nuts, lightly toasted
- 1 pound ground chuck
- 6 cloves garlic, peeled, minced
- Freshly ground pepper to taste
- Canola oil, to fry, as required

Directions:

1. For shell: Add all the ingredients for the shell into the food processor bowl. Blend until smooth. Transfer into a bowl.

2. For filling: Place a nonstick skillet over medium heat. Add olive oil. Once heated, add onions and garlic. Stir often and cook until brown. Stir in the meat, cinnamon, pepper, salt, and allspice. Cook until brown. Break the meat simultaneously as it cooks.

3. Remove from heat and add pine nuts. Mix well.

4. Make 2 tablespoons portions of the shell mixture. Shape them into balls.

5. Take one ball and place it on one of your palms. Flatten the ball using your other hand.

6. Keep a tablespoon of the filling in the middle of the flattened shell mixture. Bring the edges together and shape into a ball. This is kibbeh.

7. Repeat steps 5-6 and make the remaining kibbeh.

8. Place a deep pan over medium-high heat. Pour enough oil into the pan so that it is about 2 inches in height from the bottom of the pan.

9. When the oil is well-heated and not smoking, at about 375° F, add a few of the kibbeh.

10. Cook until golden brown all over. Do not stir too frequently initially as they can break. Remove and place on a plate.

11. Fry the remaining kibbeh similarly.

TAHINI SESAME KALE CHIPS

Serves: 12-15

Ingredients:

- 2 bunches kale, discard hard stems and ribs, torn
- 4 tablespoons olive oil
- 2 teaspoons crushed red pepper flakes (optional)
- 2 tablespoons sesame seeds
- 4 tablespoons lime juice
- 8 tablespoons tahini paste
- ¼ teaspoon salt or to taste
- ¼ teaspoon pepper or to taste

Directions:

1. Set aside the kale and add the rest of the ingredients into a large bowl. Mix well.

2. Add kale and mix well with your hands until kale is well-coated with the mixture.

3. Spread on 1-2 large baking sheets that are lined with parchment paper.

4. Bake in a preheated oven at 175° F for about an hour or until light brown and crisp. Keep a watch over the chips after about 45-50 minutes of baking as they can burn.

CHAPTER 8

ISRAELI DESSERT RECIPES

KANAFA

Serves: 16

Ingredients:
- 2 boxes (16 ounces each) frozen, shredded phyllo dough (also called kataifi)
- 2 cups shredded mozzarella cheese
- 24 ounces unsalted butter
- 2 containers (15 ounces each) ricotta cheese
- 2/3 cup white sugar

For syrup:
- 2 cups white sugar
- 2 teaspoons lemon juice
- 1 cup water
- ¼ teaspoon rose water (optional but recommended)

Directions:
1. Open the packets of shredded phyllo dough and add it into the food processor bowl.

2. Process until rice-like in texture.

3. Transfer into a large bowl.

4. Add ricotta, sugar, and mozzarella into another bowl and mix well.

5. Place butter in a microwave safe bowl that has a spout. Cook on high for about a minute or until it fully melts and foamy.

6. Remove the bowl from the microwave and let it rest for about 10 minutes. Some foam will be visible on top. Remove the foam with a spoon and discard it.

7. Add melted butter to the phyllo dough. Do not add any sediment that is present in the bottom of the bowl.

8. Mix well using your hands; for this, take some dough and rub it well between your palms. This is done to incorporate the butter well. Do this several times.

9. Take 2 large baking dishes (9 x 13 inches each). Divide the dough into the baking dishes. Press the dough well onto the bottom of the dishes.

10. Divide equally the cheese mixture over the phyllo dough layer, but do not place along the edges. Spread it evenly but leave a border of about ½-inch all around the dish.

11. Place in a preheated oven. Bake at 350° F for 30-35 minutes or until light golden brown on top and brown on the edges. Bake in batches if required.

12. Meanwhile, make the syrup as follows: Pour water into a saucepan. Add sugar and place the saucepan over medium-high heat.

13. As it starts to boil, reduce the heat to medium. Add lemon juice and stir until sugar dissolves completely and the syrup is slightly thick. Turn off the heat and add rose water. Mix well and keep it aside.

14. Remove the baking dish from the oven. Invert onto serving plates, so that now you have the cheese layer at the bottom and the phyllo crust layer on top.

15. Drizzle the syrup on the phyllo crust layer. Cut into squares and serve right away.

BAKLAVA

Serves: 18

Ingredients:

For Baklava:

- ¾ pound phyllo dough, thawed
- ½ cup sugar
- ½ teaspoon ground cloves
- 1 ½ teaspoons ground cinnamon
- 1 ½ cups butter, melted
- 1 ½ pound chopped nuts (pistachios or almonds or walnuts or use a mixture)

For the syrup:

- 1 ½ cups sugar
- 1 ½ cups water
- 1 cup honey
- 2 cinnamon sticks
- ½ teaspoon lemon juice
- Ground pistachios, to garnish (optional but recommended)

Directions:

1. Finely chop the nuts in the food processor bowl. Transfer into a bowl. Add sugar, cloves, and cinnamon and stir.

2. Unroll the dough and cut the sheets if desired to fit into the baking dish. Cover with a moist towel. This is necessary or the sheets tend to dry.

3. Pull out a sheet of dough and place on the bottom of a large baking dish (9 x 13 inches).

4. Brush with butter. Place one more sheet over this.

5. Repeat the layers (previous step until you have 8 layers in all).

6. Spread a thin layer of the chopped nuts, all over the last layer after brushing the last layer with butter.

7. Place 2 phyllo sheets over the nut layer, brushing butter on each layer.

8. Repeat steps 7-8 until all the nut mixture is used up.

9. Now place 8 more phyllo sheets over this, brushing each layer with butter. The topmost layer should also be brushed with butter. Cut into 18 equal pieces (diamond shape).

10. Place the baking dish in a preheated oven and bake at 350° F for 30-35 minutes or until light golden brown on top and light brown and crisp on the edges.

11. Meanwhile, prepare the syrup as follows: Add all the ingredients for syrup into a saucepan. Place over medium heat and bring to a boil. Now simmer on low heat for 5-6 minutes. Stir frequently until sugar melts.

12. Lower the heat and simmer until slightly thick. Turn off the heat and cool completely. Remove from the oven.

13. Discard the cinnamon stick from the cooled syrup. Pour the syrup all over the top layer.

14. Let the baklava cool completely.

15. Sprinkle pistachio nuts on top and serve.

ISRAELI CHOCOLATE RUGELACH

Serves: 9-10

Ingredients:

For dough:
- 3.5 ounces butter
- 2 tablespoons sugar
- 1 cup all-purpose flour
- 4 ounces cream cheese
- ½ teaspoon vanilla extract

For chocolate filling:
- ½ tablespoon cocoa
- 4 tablespoons sugar
- 2 tablespoons butter, melted
- ½ tablespoon ground cinnamon
- ¼ cup grated bitter-sweet chocolate

To brush:
- 2 tablespoons sugar
- 1 small egg

Directions:
1. Beat cream cheese and butter in a mixing bowl with an electric hand mixer until creamy.

2. Beat in the vanilla and sugar. Beat until creamy and light.

3. Add flour and stir lightly into dough. Chill for at least an hour.

4. To make filling: Add cocoa, sugar, cinnamon, and chocolate into a bowl and stir.

5. Divide the mixture into 2 equal portions and shape into balls.

6. Dust your countertop with some flour. Place a ball of dough and roll into a round shape of around 1/8-inch thickness.

7. Brush some melted butter in the middle of the rolled dough, leaving a ½-inch border all around. Spread some chocolate mixture over the buttered area. Cut into wedges with a pizza cutter. The wide end of the wedge should be 1-1 ½ inches wide.

8. Separate the wedges from each other. Roll each wedge, from the wide side toward the thinner side to the tip of the wedge. Place on a lined baking sheet, with the seam side facing down.

9. For brushing: Add sugar and egg into a bowl and whisk well.

10. Brush the top of the rolls with egg mixture.

11. Repeat steps 6-10 with the other ball of dough.

12. Place the baking dish in a preheated oven and bake at 350° F for 30-35 minutes or until golden brown on top.

13. Remove from the oven and cool completely. Store in an airtight container.

TAHINI OLIVE OIL CAKE

Serves: Makes one cake.

Ingredients:
- 1 cup extra-virgin olive oil
- 1 cup sugar
- 4 tablespoons lemon juice
- 1 cup honey
- 1 cup Sabra classic tahini
- 4 tablespoons grated lemon zest

For dry ingredients:
- 3 cups all-purpose flour
- ½ teaspoon salt
- 1 teaspoon baking soda
- 2 teaspoons baking powder
- ½ teaspoon ground nutmeg
- 2 teaspoons ground cinnamon
- 1 teaspoon ground cardamom

To serve:
- Whipped cream
- Honey
- Grated lemon zest
- Fresh raspberries

Directions:

1. Grease a large, round baking dish (9-10 inches) with some oil and place a sheet of parchment paper inside the baking dish. Grease the parchment paper as well.

2. Add honey, sugar, and oil into the mixing bowl of the stand mixer. Beat until very smooth.

3. Beat in the Sabra Classic Tahini, lemon zest, and lemon juice.

4. Mix together all the dry ingredients in another bowl.

5. Mix together the dry ingredients and wet ingredients and beat until just incorporated.

6. Transfer the batter into the prepared baking dish.

7. Bake in an oven that has been preheated previously at 350° F for 30 to 35 minutes or until brown on top and the cake is set in the middle.

8. Cool completely on your countertop. Cover the cake with a foil tent loosely until use.

9. Top with the suggested serving options. Cut into slices and serve.

BASBOUSA-SEMOLINA CAKE SOAKED IN LEMON ROSEWATER SYRUP

Serves: 8-12

Ingredients:

For Basbousa:
- 1½ cups semolina
- 2 teaspoon baking powder
- 8 tablespoons butter, softened
- 4 tablespoons sugar
- 1 cup all-purpose flour
- 2 eggs
- 1 cup whole milk yogurt
- Almonds, to garnish

For the syrup:
- 1 cup sugar
- 1 ½ cups water
- 4-5 teaspoons lime or lemon juice
- 2 teaspoons rose water
- 2 tablespoons freshly grated lemon or orange lime zest

Directions:
1. Add semolina, baking powder, and flour into a bowl and mix until well-combined.

2. Stir in the eggs, sugar, yogurt, and butter and beat well with a hand mixer until just incorporated. Do not beat for too long.

3. Spoon the mixture into a greased microwave-safe dish.

4. Top with almonds. Place them in such a manner that once you cut the baked cake, each serving gets an almond.

5. Cover the dish with plastic wrap.

6. Cook on high in the microwave for 5 minutes. Keep a watch on the cake after 4 minutes. The cake should not be very dry.

7. To make syrup: Meanwhile, add water and sugar into a saucepan. Place the saucepan on medium heat. Once it starts boiling, simmer for 10-12 minutes on low heat.

8. Remove from heat and lemon juice, zest, and rosewater. Mix well.

9. Cool and pour over the baked basbousa. Let it cool to room temperature.

10. Cut into squares and serve.

CONCLUSION

Thank you once again for purchasing the book.

If you are into Israeli cooking and want to whip something up, you can use the recipes in this book, and in no time, you will cook an authentic Israeli meal. There are numerous recipes in this book for different meals during the day. The recipes are delicious, and the instructions in the book are simple to follow.

By the end of the book, you can confidently call yourself a master chef at Israeli cooking.

I hope you and your family enjoy the delicious, mouthwatering recipes in this book.

Made in the USA
Las Vegas, NV
18 January 2024

84512911R00090